THE WORLD SHE IMAGINES WITH HIM

SOUNDARYA. K.

Copyright © Soundarya. K.
All Rights Reserved.

ISBN 979-888606544-2

Contents

About The Author

She is Soundarya.k. She is a budding writer. She belongs to Erode district. She completed her Master's in English Literature. She loves to read books. Her passion is to be a writer. She is the co-author of the book VOW OF YOUTH. To admire her works,
Follow her at INSTAGRAM: soundurithi
EMAIL; soundudinu@gmail.com.

ONE

AWAKENED NIGHTS

The night that fall,

Making my thoughts ,

To go so far.

The dreams that raise,

With open eyes,

Shrinking my heart.

Provoking my dreams,

With mystic

Dreams and Thoughts.

The flow of dreams,

Binding my eyes,

Not to fall asleep.

With your memories,

Drowning in the night,

Without sleep.

TWO

THE DAY I HOLD YOUR HANDS

From the day I am with you,

I wanna hold my pen,

Till the demise of mine,

To inscribe in each page,

The warmth of love,

We hold together.

THREE

THE WORLD I IMAGINE WITH YOU

Day or Night,

I wanna shut my eyes,

The dream that knocks,

Makes me delight,

The world I imagine,

Where I am being with you,

Holding hands together,

Never wanna shut my eyes,

Until,

I make it forever.

FOUR

AT ONE MOONLIGHT WITH YOU

The darkest night,

Alluring moonlight,

The calm refreshing breeze,

The enchanting nature,

But I kept my sight aside,

Far from all the delights,

Looking for my honey bee,

To me, at my side.

FIVE
ETERNAL LOVE

You were by my side,

At the time I cried,

The pain I held,

Couldn't be revealed,

The words of yours,

Drenched my soul,

With eternal love.

SIX

I AM MAD ABOUT YOU

With madness,

Scribbled some letters,

My eyes,

Sparkled with joy,

As I found,

It's the name of yours.

SEVEN

THE DAY I GET DOWN ON ONE KNEE

The day,

I get down on knees,

To make a proposal,

Accord you,

Not the roses,

Instead the poems,

Which echoes,

The love of mine.

EIGHT

HIS BEWITCHING LOOKS

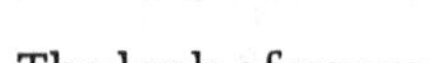

The look of yours,

Bewitched my soul,

Gravitating me,

Throughout the day,

To look at you,

And fall,

Again and again.

NINE

MY POEMS SOUNDS MY LOVE ALOUD

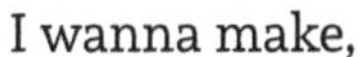

I wanna make,

Not the history,

But the memory,

My soul,

Which is mortal,

Want my love,

To be immortal,

I make my love,

Sounds aloud,

Through the poems,

Of mine.

TEN

THOUGHTS OF YOURS BINDED ME FOREVER

The Sun,

In a day,

It itself has its boundary,

To rise and set,

Whereas you,

Binded me,

With your,

Unbounded thoughts.

ELEVEN

MY LOVE FOR YOU WHICH IS UNHEARD

I am not a Sculptor,

But I carve.

Not to make the world,

To Look Awe,

Want not to be praised,

Else sink in my own world,

Where I love to,

Pen down my emotions,

Which is Unheard.

TWELVE

TODAY'S VAIN; TOMORROW'S GAIN

Dark clouds.

Makes the star visible,

Bright clouds,

Makes the star invisible,

The strenuous circumstance,

Trigger to blaze,

Today's melancholy,

The next day's gay,

The person of today.

The personality of tomorrow.

THIRTEEN
THE SECOND I SEE YOU

You are the one,

To whom I am longing,

The second I see you,

It cherishes me with pleasure,

The words of yours,

Fills me with love,

The moment you part, I feel like,

Something I have lost,

But Its you.

FOURTEEN

HER SECRET DIARY

He is her secret diary,

Which nods for all the

Trashes she hold,

Which bends for All her emotions,

He is her special toy,

Her convenient shoulder To lie on,

His warmth of hug Is her secret shelter,

His cold lips made,

Her minutes to freeze,

She endured the minutes,

SOUNDARYA. K.

To be together

www.ingramcontent.com/pod-product-compliance
Lightning Source LLC
Chambersburg PA
CBHW072147150726
48002CB00004B/1661